THE FASCINATING WORLD OF ELEPHANTS

JUAN PIMENTEL

Juan Pimentel was born in La Vega, Dominican Republic. Known for his writing prowess, broadcasting skills, and ability to create highly influential content, he has been especially prominent in the Social Security and Retirement space in the United States. Juan has managed to enrich and strengthen the Spanish-speaking community with his valuable information. We invite you to join us on this captivating journey through The Fantastic World of Elephants, second edition!

For more information, visit the author's website: www.JuanPimentel.com

CHAPTERS

Prologue

In the confines of the vast earth, where nature still reigns in its most majestic splendor, giants walk with serene steps. Its imposing shapes are silhouetted against the horizon, reminding us of the greatness of wildlife and the wonder of the biodiversity that inhabits our planet. These giants are elephants, beings whose stories have been intertwined with ours since time immemorial.

From African savannahs to Asian forests, elephants have captured our imagination and respect throughout history. Their presence evokes a sense of wonder and admiration that transcends cultural and geographic boundaries. But beyond their mere presence, these beings have a fascinating story to tell, a story of evolution, adaptation and coexistence in a constantly changing world.

In the pages that follow, we will explore the deepest corners of elephant life. From their intricate anatomies and elaborate forms of communication to their surprising intelligence and complex social structures, we will discover how these beings intertwine with ecosystems.

But this trip will not only immerse us in the life of elephants; It will also confront us with the threatening realities we face in an ever-changing modern world. Poaching for precious ivory, habitat loss and conflicts with human communities are challenges that require our urgent attention.

As we delve into this exploration, I invite you to discover the beauty and complexity of the world of elephants. Through their eyes and experiences, we can better understand our connection to the natural realm and the importance of preserving the diversity of life in all its forms. May this journey inspire us to take action, to appreciate and protect these majestic giants, and to honor our responsibility as guardians of this planet we all share.

Welcome to "Majestic Giants: The Fascinating World of Elephants."

I DEDICATE THIS BOOK TO MY
MOTHER, A BEACON OF LOVE
AND STRENGTH IN MY LIFE.

Chapter 1
Introduction to Elephants

Elephants are majestic and enigmatic creatures that roam with grace and power through the vast expanses of land and lush forests of various continents, they have exerted a deep-rooted attraction on the human imagination throughout the centuries. Their imposing presence, defying gravity itself with every step they take, is just the beginning of their captivating nature.

From ancient times to modern days, elephants have been an object of fascination and veneration in numerous cultures around the world. In many societies, these majestic giants have been symbols of strength, wisdom and power. Their iconic silhouettes and distinctive horns, so versatile in their uses, have captured the imagination of artists, poets and writers throughout history, inspiring epic tales and legends that have endured through generations.

Gifted with astonishing intelligence and deeply complex social behavior, elephants represent a unique example of sophistication in the animal kingdom.

However, beyond their impact on culture and art, elephants have also been protagonists in the evolution and development of the natural world. As we explore the history of these impressive animals, we delve into the fascinating saga of their evolution over countless generations.

From their prehistoric ancestors to modern species, elephants have gone through a process of change and adaptation that has led to the formation of the different species we know today.

Elephants' ancestral ties to the ancient mammals that populated prehistoric eras offer us a window into our planet's distant past.

As we unravel their evolutionary history, we discover how these magnificent beings have survived and thrived in diverse environments over millions of years, adapting to climate changes and transformations on Earth that would have challenged many other species.

This first chapter of our exploration barely scratches the surface of the fascinating elephant narrative. As we immerse ourselves in their history and unique characteristics, we embark on a journey of discovery that will lead us to a deeper understanding of the importance of these creatures in the very fabric of life on Earth.

As we delve into elephant intelligence and learning, we are faced with a cognitive maze full of wonders. Each discovery brings us closer to understanding the richness of their minds and the way intelligence has been a fundamental tool in their journey through evolution.

The incomparable wealth of biodiversity that adorns our planet is manifested in a truly impressive way through the three main species of elephants that have made their home in various corners of the earth.

African savanna elephants (Loxodonta Africana) emerge as majestic creatures that spark the imagination with their imposing wingspan and characteristic ears that, on many occasions, seem to reflect the very silhouette of the African continent they call home.

These magnificent colossi have conquered the vast expanses of the African plains, where their mere presence not only shapes the landscape, but also exerts a deep-rooted influence on the delicate balance of the surrounding ecosystem.

Their footprints in the earth seem to tell ancestral stories of life and survival in one of the most captivating environments in the world. In a fascinating contrast, African forest elephants (Loxodonta cyclotis) present a more modest, but equally intriguing picture.

These inhabitants of the dense forests that trace their path through central and western Africa are a living manifestation of the admirable evolutionary adaptation to environments characterized by perpetual gloom and lush humidity.

Their rounded ears and more compact size are a visual testament to how nature, in its relentless process of refinement, has shaped these creatures to thrive in the most challenging circumstances.

Every step they take on the jungle floor is a palpable reminder of the astonishing diversity of life and evolution's ability to sculpt beings that adapt and flourish in the most specific and seemingly inhospitable niches.

However, the amazing journey through the world of elephants does not stop there. On the other side of the globe, in the lush reaches of Asia, Asian elephants (Elephas maximus) have woven a highly unique relationship with the region's peaceful mountain landscapes and lush jungles.

With smaller ears and a straight shape, these elephants exhibit a surprising level of intelligence and a unique ability to interact closely with the human cultures that have been an integral part of their environment throughout history.

Their contributions to people's lives, from assisting with agricultural tasks to playing an emblematic role in festivities and rituals, have left their mark both on the land and in the stories of those who share their world.

Elephants share an ancestral lineage with extinct creatures, such as the imposing mammoths and colossal mastodons. As we explore the lines traced by their evolution, a unique window unfolds before us that connects us directly to the remote eras when prehistoric mammals reigned supreme on Earth.

By tracing their origins, we discover that modern elephants are living bearers of this history spanning millions of years. Our current elephants are not only witnesses of the past, but also guardians of ancestral legacies.

In the depths of their genetic structure and in the way they manifest today, we find reminiscences of their ancestors who populated a varied range of habitats and regions, contributing to the diversity of life that unfolded throughout different geological eras.

The multiplicity of species and subspecies of elephants presents us with a mosaic of adaptations and parallel evolution that has occurred over eons.

The multiplicity of species and subspecies of elephants presents us with a mosaic of adaptations and parallel evolution that has occurred over eons.

Each elephant, with its distinctive morphological characteristics and unique behaviors, tells its own evolutionary story. From the vast African plains to the dense Asian jungles, these majestic creatures have been shaped by the relentless force of natural selection and the changing conditions of their environment.

The footprint of elephants in human history extends far beyond biological limits, delicately woven into the same fibers that make up the culture, religion and identity of diverse civilizations.

Over the centuries, these magnificent beings have transcended their mere animal existence to transform into potent symbols of power, wisdom and spirituality, leaving an indelible mark on the hearts and minds of people around the world.

Throughout the recesses of history, elephants have played a vital role in the fabric of cultural and religious life. In numerous Asian civilizations, elephants have been considered ambassadors of good fortune, bearers of authority and guardians of spiritual mysteries.

 Their majestic presence has become intertwined with divine figures and significant events, granting them a special place in cultural and religious narratives. From ancient India to Buddhist temples in Thailand, elephants have been revered as beings that embody the very essence of nobility and the connection between the material and spiritual worlds.

No less important is their impact on the African continent, where elephants have also left a deep mark on myths and traditions.

In this vast territory, these majestic creatures embody the indomitable force of nature, reminding us of the intrinsic fragility and resilience of life on Earth.

EPISODE 2
ANATOMY AND PHYSIOLOGY

Elephants, with their imposing presence that defies gravity with every step, introduce us to a world of extraordinary dimensions. The majesty of its anatomy reveals evolutionary adaptation to diverse and challenging environments.

The Essential Trunk: The trunk, a masterful fusion of nose and upper lip, is not only a hallmark of elephants, but also an essential multifunctional tool. With more than 40,000 muscles, the trunk is the key to its survival, using it to feed, drink, communicate and express emotions. Its versatility in the use of the trunk highlights the sophistication of its evolution.

Elephants Tusks not only represent a genetic heritage shared with illustrious ancestors, such as the majestic mammoths, but they also witness a constant challenge in the trajectory of elephants. More than just dental appendages, these tusks have been invaluable companions in elephants' daily lives, used deftly to dig up water, tear off bark, and engage in intricate social interactions.

These tusks, however, have gone from being functional elements to symbols of beauty and, unfortunately, threats to the survival of elephants.

Relentless poaching for ivory has sparked an unequal struggle, endangering the very existence of these incredible animals. Each tusk, which should be a masterpiece of nature, has become a coveted treasure that has led to the ruthless persecution of elephants in their natural habitat.

The urgency of conservation measures becomes evident when we contemplate the magnitude of the threat elephants face due to poaching. Conservation is not just a matter of protecting a species; It is an act of preserving the evolutionary history that these tusks carry with them.

Each elephant with intact tusks is a living testament to the long and fascinating history of its species, a history that spans geological eras and is intrinsically intertwined with the evolution of life on Earth.

Ears, more than mere anatomical appendages, are true evolutionary wonders in African and Asian elephants, revealing the richness of the adaptation of these majestic giants to diverse environments.

The ears, large and distinctive in African elephants, are not only aesthetic elements that contribute to their majestic presence, but also play a crucial role in their thermal regulation. These appendages, beyond their obvious usefulness in hearing, act as sophisticated temperature regulators.

In the vast African landscapes, where the sun can be relentless, the wide ears act as natural radiators, dissipating heat and keeping elephants cool. This example of adaptation shows how each anatomical trait has been shaped by natural selection to guarantee survival in its habitat.

In contrast, Asian elephants, inhabitants of dense and humid forests, have more rounded and compact ears. This adaptation is an evolutionary response to an environment where thermal regulation is not as crucial as on the African plains. The different shape and size of their ears reflect the diversity of environmental challenges they have faced throughout the ages.

The feet of the elephants, large and padded, are not only witnesses of an amazing evolutionary engineering, but also of a fundamental adaptation to move in silence through their surroundings. The efficient distribution of weight and its massive extremities not only minimizes the environmental impact, but also allows them to move gracefully and quietly through the undergrowth and dense vegetation.

Every step they take, with their feet designed to distribute weight evenly, is a testament to how evolution has sculpted not only form but also function. In the silent environments of jungles or grasslands, this adaptation not only guarantees the efficiency of the hunt or the search for food, but also gives elephants a tactical advantage when moving stealthily.

The relationship between elephants' ears and feet forms a symphony of adaptation, each note telling the story of how these animals have thrived in diverse environments.

From the vast African plains to the dense Asian jungles, each variation in the anatomy of these adaptive organs is a response to the specific challenges of their habitats.

The dentition of elephants stands as an evolutionary masterpiece that goes beyond being a simple anatomical detail; It is an efficient system in constant replacement, revealing the extraordinary adaptation of these majestic animals to a specific herbivorous diet.

Each molar in an elephant's mouth is more than a tooth; It is a testament to their unique ability to meet the challenges of their environment. Adapted to a herbivorous diet, elephants have perfected a dental system that is constantly worn down and renewed. This cyclical process is essential for extracting nutrients from the harder plant fibers that make up your daily diet.

Elephant dentition is not static; It is a constant dance of attrition and regeneration. Each molar that wears out is replaced by a new one in a continuous process throughout its life. This evolutionary adaptation ensures that elephants can cope with the demands of a fibrous and abrasive diet, ensuring that they always have the necessary tools to extract essential nutrients from their food.

Each tooth that is replaced is not only a functional component of an elephant's dentition, but also a testament to its resilience and adaptability. Through millions of years of evolution, these animals have perfected their dental systems to survive in diverse environments, from the African plains to the dense Asian jungles.

The intimate relationship between elephants' herbivorous diet and their dental system is a striking example of evolutionary specialization. Their molars, designed to crush and grind tough vegetation, reflect the harmony between form and function in nature. Each tooth is a tool adapted to extract the maximum nutritional value from its varied diet.

Efficient elephant dentition is not only a biological phenomenon; It is a life cycle in constant renewal. From infancy to old age, each elephant experiences this process, marking not only its physical development, but also its ability to evolve and thrive in an ever-changing world.

The ability of elephants to digest their fibrous diet stands as a marvel of evolutionary adaptation, a biological phenomenon that goes beyond mere food intake.

The efficiency of their digestive system, especially the ingenious design of their large intestine, acts as a decomposition and fermentation machine, allowing these majestic animals to extract essential nutrients from plant materials that might be inaccessible to other herbivores.

The large intestine of elephants is not simply a part of their anatomy; is a biological factory masterfully designed for the decomposition and fermentation of plant fibers.

This evolutionary adaptation allows elephants to extract essential nutrients from difficult-to-digest materials, turning their fibrous diet into a rich and sustainable source of energy.

Each stage of the process, from initial decomposition to nutrient absorption, is a dance orchestrated by evolution to ensure the survival and prosperity of these giant herbivores.

Elephant digestion is like a biological ballet, a choreography of processes that occur with precision. Bacteria in the large intestine break down plant fibers, releasing essential nutrients in the fermentation process. This biological ballet is not only a testament to evolutionary adaptation, but also a specific response to the challenges of its habitat.

In environments where food availability can be variable, the ability to extract maximum nutritional value from even the toughest plant materials gives elephants a crucial advantage in the fight for survival.

Elephant digestion also becomes a lesson in biological sustainability. Its ability to make the most of available food resources highlights the efficiency of the food chain and the interconnection of elements in an ecosystem.

In a world where sustainability is increasingly crucial, elephants are presented as living examples of how nature has sculpted evolutionary strategies to ensure long-term survival.

Every aspect of elephant digestion is a page in the evolutionary book, a narrative of how nature has sculpted these animals to thrive in diverse environments.

From the challenges of the African plains to the dense Asian jungles, evolution has equipped elephants with specific biological tools that have made them experts at extracting nutrients from their environment.

Elephants' measured breathing is more than a physiological function; It is a silent symphony of adaptation and survival.

Every inhalation and exhalation resonates with the ability of these animals to meet challenges over millions of years. This symphony has been perfected over time, an evolutionary response to the need to adapt to constantly changing environments.

This journey through elephant anatomy and physiology is, in itself, an odyssey toward a deeper understanding of these amazing creatures. Every anatomical detail, from trunk to tusks, from ears to feet, becomes a portal that transports us through the ages and allows us to witness the living history of elephants.

The low metabolic rate of elephants, compared to that of other large mammals, is not simply a statistic; It is a slow pace of life that contributes to its longevity. This metabolic efficiency allows them to conserve energy and maintain a subtle balance between activity and rest.

CHAPTER 3
BEHAVIOR AND SOCIAL LIFE

The social behavior of elephants is worthy of admiration due to their outstanding capacity for cooperation. These majestic animals not only live in herds, but also show an amazing willingness to collaborate in making crucial decisions that affect the survival and well-being of the entire group.

In particular, fundamental decisions, such as searching for water or choosing migratory routes, are approached by elephants through complex interactions and consensus formation. This process reveals a form of exceptional social intelligence, where individuals actively consider the needs and preferences of the group before reaching a joint decision.

Cooperative decision-making among elephants is not only a testament to their social cunning, but also a vital mechanism for strengthening herd unity and ensuring their survival in challenging environments.

This social intelligence not only translates into practical benefits, but also highlights the complexity of interindividual relationships in the animal kingdom, challenging our perceptions about the cognitive ability of non-human species. In short, the cooperation and consensual decision-making among elephants underscores the depth of their social intelligence, offering a fascinating insight into the complexity of social dynamics in the animal kingdom.

Knowledge transfer emerges as a crucial pillar in the social life of elephants. Throughout generations, experiences are shared and taught, leading to the accumulation of invaluable collective wisdom. Migration routes, water sources, and foraging tactics are meticulously transmitted through observation and imitation, ensuring the pack's continued adaptability to ever-changing environments.

This touching behavior further highlights the sophistication of social relationships among elephants, and challenges the traditional belief that certain emotional aspects are unique to humans.

 Elephants' ability to express comfort and empathy provides a fascinating glimpse into the depth of their social connections and complex emotional lives, challenging our preconceived perceptions about the nature of intelligence and sentience in the animal kingdom. In short, the social life of elephants is revealed to be an intricate web of shared emotions and acts of support, highlighting the surprising sophistication of their social world.

Festivities and social rituals, far from being mere manifestations of joy, emerge as essential components in the social cohesion of elephants. It is in these significant events, such as the birth of a calf, where festive gestures are displayed that transcend mere celebration and become powerful mechanisms for strengthening emotional ties within the pack.

These rituals, often filled with symbolism and emotion, reflect a rich and complex emotional range, serving as testimony to the deep social connection that characterizes the lives of elephants.

When a new calf enters the world, the pack joins in a collective celebration, expressing their joy in ways that go beyond the simple expression of joy.

These festive gestures not only underline the importance of the event itself, but also act as powerful catalysts to strengthen social bonds between pack members. Active participation in these rituals not only fosters unity, but also contributes to the construction of a more intricate and robust emotional fabric within the elephant community.

It is in these significant events, such as the birth of a calf, where festive gestures are displayed that transcend mere celebration and become powerful mechanisms for strengthening emotional ties within the pack.

As we delve into the fascinating world of diverse elephant species, it becomes clear and compelling that their complex social behaviors have evolved in surprisingly adaptive ways to address the specific challenges of their respective environments.

This adaptability is, in fact, eloquent proof of the ability of these majestic creatures to develop specialized strategies that allow them to not only survive, but thrive, in their varied habitats.

On the vast plains of the African savannah, for example, we see how collaboration becomes a fundamental pillar of the social life of African elephants.

The need to face challenges such as searching for water and protection from predators has shaped the evolution of cooperative strategies. Here, African elephants have honed the ability to work together, demonstrating an impressive ability to make collective decisions that benefit the entire herd.

On the other hand, in the dense and lush Asian jungles, stealthy mobility emerges as an essential strategy to face the challenges of a more closed and complex habitat. Asian elephant species have developed a surprising skill at moving silently through the dense jungle, adapting their social behaviors to maximize efficiency in searching for food and avoiding potential threats.

In short, the exploration of the behavior and social life of elephants leads us to a fascinating realm, where cooperation, empathy and celebration emerge as essential foundations.

These magnificent creatures have not only stood the test of time, but have thrived on the strength of their community bonds. As we immerse ourselves in the pages of this narrative, we will embark on a journey that goes beyond simple observation; It will be a continuous discovery of the secrets and wonders that define the social fabric of elephants.

This story invites us to more deeply unravel the
mysteries that surround these amazing beings,
immersing us in a fascinating world of
interpersonal relationships and unique
behaviors. The life of elephants, far from simple
survival, is a vibrant tapestry of shared
experiences, intertwined emotions and
moments of celebration that have withstood
the tests of time.

As we progress through these pages, a journey
awaits us into the very heart of the elephant
community, where every detail reveals the
extraordinary complexity of their social
existence. Are you ready to delve into these
pages full of wonders and reveal the mysteries
that await? This book invites you to join the
expedition, promising a deep dive into the
fascinating world of elephants, where each
chapter will reveal new layers of understanding
and wonder. Get ready for a unique experience
that will transform your perspective on these
magnificent beings!

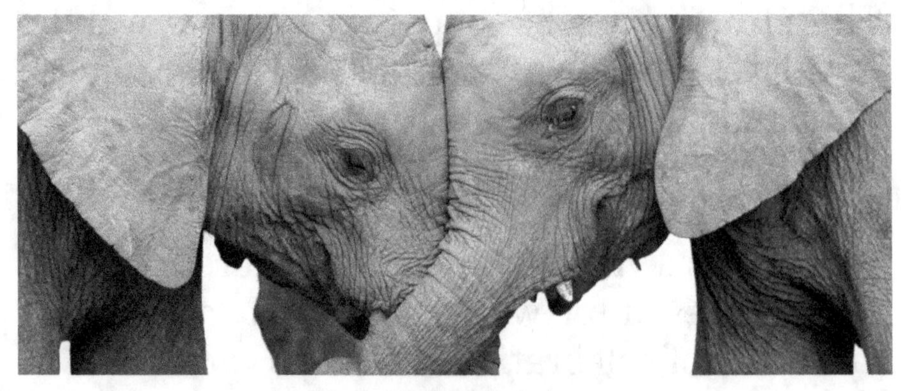

Chapter 4
Intelligence and Learning

Elephant intelligence is emerging as a fascinating phenomenon that not only constitutes a distinctive trait, but is revealed as a crucial tool for their survival in a wide variety of environments. Over millions of years of evolution and adaptation, these majestic animals have developed an extraordinary capacity for problem-solving and strategic decision-making, giving them a significant adaptive advantage in their complex and changing habitat.

Each manifestation of elephant intelligence reflects an intricate web of cognitive and social abilities. Your ability to solve problems goes beyond simply executing simple tasks; It implies a level of abstract thought that distinguishes them in the animal kingdom.

We watch as they use improvised tools, such as branches or stones, to achieve specific goals, demonstrating amazing creativity and adaptability.

Likewise, strategic decision making plays a crucial role in the lives of elephants, especially in situations involving foraging, resource management, and herd protection. Their ability to plan and coordinate complex activities, as well as to remember and learn from past experiences, critically contributes to their success in survival over time.

This impressive display of intelligence is not only manifested at the individual level, but also in the complexity of social interactions within the pack. Elephants are deeply social animals that develop strong family bonds and demonstrate empathy and cooperation.

The transmission of knowledge and experience between generations, combined with complex and subtle communication, highlights the richness of their social intelligence.

Elephant intelligence is presented as a fascinating phenomenon that not only serves as a distinctive trait, but also reveals itself as an absolutely crucial tool for their survival in an astonishing variety of environments. Through millions of years of evolution and adaptation, these majestic mammals have developed an extraordinary ability to address a wide range of challenges, from solving everyday problems to making large-scale strategic decisions.

Every manifestation of elephant intelligence has been forged in the crucible of evolution, shaped by the constant need to meet and overcome the changing challenges of their environment. Your problem-solving ability is not limited to simple tasks; it goes further, involving abstract thinking that highlights its unique position in the animal kingdom.

Elephants have demonstrated amazing abilities in using improvised tools, such as branches or stones, to achieve specific goals, underscoring their exceptional level of creativity and adaptability.

Strategic decision-making stands as a fundamental pillar in the lives of elephants, especially in contexts that encompass foraging, resource management and safeguarding the herd. Their ability to plan and coordinate complex activities, as well as to remember and learn from past experiences, contributes essentially to their adaptive success and survival throughout the ages.

This impressive display of intelligence is not only manifested at the individual level; It is also reflected in the complexity of social interactions within the pack. Elephants are deeply social animals that develop strong family bonds and exhibit empathetic and cooperative behaviors. The transmission of knowledge and experience between generations, combined with complex and nuanced communication, highlights the richness of their social intelligence.

Remarkable beings in the animal kingdom, elephants display truly exceptional problem-solving skills, tackling complex challenges with a masterful combination of ingenuity and adaptability.

A close examination of their behaviors reveals a fascinating panorama of cognitive abilities that have evolved over millions of years to provide these majestic mammals with a unique ability to cope with various situations in their environment.

Meticulous observations in the wild have provided valuable insights into how elephants use improvised tools to overcome obstacles and achieve specific goals. From the use of artfully selected branches to the strategic use of stones, these animals have demonstrated amazing dexterity in using unconventional objects, underscoring their innate ability to think creatively and solve problems efficiently.

Creativity in problem solving is not only limited to physical tools, but also manifests in their collaboration and coordination strategies within the pack.

 Close observation of social interactions among elephants reveals the complexity of their social intelligence, where subtle communication and strategic collaboration play a crucial role in resolving problematic situations, such as searching for food or protecting the most vulnerable members. .

Throughout the vast history of humanity, the prodigious memory of elephants has been a constant source of admiration and amazement. Scientific research has delved into this fascinating characteristic, shedding light on the notorious ability of these majestic mammals to retain information over the long term.

Studies support the notion that elephants not only possess exceptional memory, but also employ it in extraordinary ways to remember migratory routes, precise locations of water sources, and intricate social relationships.

The amazing retentiveness of elephants is manifested in their detailed memories of vast territories, allowing them to make precise and strategic migrations in search of essential resources.

This knowledge embedded in memory not only gives them an adaptive advantage in changing environments, but also highlights the depth of their connection to the environment.

In addition to remembering critical geospatial data, elephants also maintain a meticulous social record in their prodigious minds. They remember not only specific individuals within their pack, but also the complexities of social relationships, hierarchies, and emotional bonds.

This social knowledge, stored and constantly updated in their memories, contributes significantly to the social cohesion of the pack, facilitating harmonious interactions and collaborative strategies.

The ability to remember past experiences and apply that knowledge in current situations gives elephants an evolutionary advantage that goes beyond mere individual survival. This exceptional memory becomes a vital component for the transmission of knowledge between generations, ensuring the continuity of successful strategies and effective adaptation to changes in the environment.

The extraordinary capacity for communication between elephants transcends the limits of sounds audible to humans, revealing a complex linguistic framework that goes beyond our perception.

These majestic mammals, endowed with a unique sensitivity, use a varied range of vocalizations, some of which include infrasound, imperceptible to our ears, but essential for the transmission of crucial information within their community.

Elephants' use of infrasound is particularly notable, as these low-frequency sounds can travel long distances and penetrate obstacles, facilitating effective communication across vast expanses of terrain. This form of communication has been observed in various contexts, from warning about the presence of predators to indicating the location of water sources or abundant food resources.

The complex communication system of elephants is not simply limited to the transmission of practical information, but also encompasses emotional expressions. Vocalizations, both audible and infrasonic, serve as a kind of emotional language that allows these animals to share emotional states, strengthening social bonds within the herd. From the expression of joy to the communication of risk situations, this linguistic network among elephants highlights the depth of their social intelligence.

The sophistication of communication between elephants not only highlights their ability to convey accurate information, but also their ability to adapt their messages to specific situations. The variability in tone, duration and frequency of their vocalizations reveals a linguistic complexity that suggests the existence of a highly developed communicative code among these majestic animals.

Elephants' recognition abilities emerge as a fascinating phenomenon that extends to both their own peers and other species, revealing a level of insight and empathy that highlights their astonishing emotional intelligence.

In numerous observations, it has been confirmed that these majestic mammals not only distinguish individualities within their herd, but also express empathy towards members who face afflictions, expressing gestures of comfort and support that demonstrate their deep understanding of the emotions and experiences of their fellow humans. .

These gestures not only underscore his ability to recognize the suffering of others, but also reveal an impressive understanding of the emotional complexities that characterize social interactions in his community.

This empathetic behavior is not just limited to members of their own species; It has been recorded on multiple occasions that elephants express surprising recognition and sensitivity towards individuals of other species.

From comforting injured animals to adopting orphaned offspring of other species, these displays of empathy transcend the barriers of biological family and reveal the breadth of their compassion and interspecific recognition.

The emotional intelligence of elephants is manifested as a fundamental pillar in the social cohesion of their herd, contributing to solid interpersonal relationships and a harmonious social structure.

Active participation in games and recreational activities also helps to foster resilience in elephants.

Through overcoming challenges and adapting
to new situations, these animals demonstrate a
remarkable ability to face adversity with
determination and flexibility. This resilience is
not only a testament to their intelligence, but
also a crucial component to their adaptation to
changing and challenging environments,
whether in the wild or in captivity.

Creativity is impressively manifested when
elephants tackle these cognitive challenges.
The way they improvise solutions, use tools, or
apply novel strategies reveals an intriguing
facet of their brilliant mind. This creativity not
only contributes to effective problem solving,
but also highlights the versatility and richness
of their intelligence, which goes beyond the
simple execution of tasks.

The ability to understand and respond to the
emotions of others not only strengthens the
bonds within the pack, but also highlights the
depth of the emotional life of these
extraordinary animals.

Elephants' outstanding intelligence is rigorously tested through a variety of cognitive challenges and games, taking place both in the wild and in captive environments.

 These challenges not only serve as mental stimuli for these majestic mammals, but also trigger a host of additional benefits, such as building resilience and stimulating creativity. Elephants, in their imposing wisdom, exhibit an innate ability to tackle complex problems with a captivating mix of curiosity and perseverance.

When subjected to games and activities designed to stimulate their mental acuity, elephants reveal additional layers of their intelligence.

Chapter 5
Eating Habits and Impact on the Ecosystem

True consummate herbivores, elephants have evolved with an exceptional affinity for a diverse diet encompassing grasses, fruits, bark and branches. This food selection not only reflects their intrinsic connection to the ecosystems they inhabit, but also highlights the adaptability and specialization of their physiological systems.

The dental structure of elephants, a marvel of natural engineering, is presented as a fundamental piece in this evolutionary adaptation that guarantees perfection in their way of feeding.

Elephants' uniquely designed molars are constantly replaced throughout their lives, a remarkable evolutionary adaptation.

This tooth replacement cycle allows them to not only grind and extract nutrients from the hardest plant fibers, but also maintain optimal dental health throughout the various stages of their existence. This continuous process of tooth regeneration is essential to ensure that elephants can make the most of their specialized diet while also meeting the wear and tear challenges associated with their feeding habit.

The dental specialization of elephants is a testament to the harmonious coevolution between their physiology and the environment. The ability to chew and process a wide variety of plant foods not only gives them an adaptive advantage in terms of survival, but also reveals the intricate relationship between elephants and the ecosystems in which they play a vital role.

Elephants' intricate relationship with vegetation goes beyond mere foraging, revealing a critical role as unwitting architects of the landscape.

Their constant movement through different areas of their habitat has a significant impact on the health and vitality of the local flora. Beyond simply being consumers of vegetation, elephants play an active role in shaping the ecosystems in which they live.

The contribution of elephants to botanical diversity is a fascinating phenomenon. By consuming a wide variety of plants, these giant herbivores become agents of change that promote the variety and abundance of plant species.

Their habit of selecting different types of vegetation during their migrations and erratic feeding patterns contributes to the heterogeneity of the landscape, enriching the botanical composition of their environment.

A particularly crucial aspect of elephants' interaction with vegetation is their role as seed dispersers.

By ingesting fruits and other plant components, elephants transport seeds through their digestive system, which are then deposited in different locations through their excrement. This seed dispersal process is essential for the natural regeneration of the environment, as it helps to establish new plants and contributes to the renewal of the landscape in a sustainable way.

The importance of this intimate interaction between elephants and vegetation highlights their fundamental role as guardians of biodiversity. They are not simply inhabitants of their environment; They are key players in the dynamics and health of the ecosystems they call home. Conservation of elephants is not only crucial for their survival but also for maintaining biological diversity and ecological balance in their natural habitats.

Elephants, in their majesty and complexity as living beings, are not limited to being simple consumers of vegetation, but play an active and transformative role in shaping the landscape they inhabit.

Their remarkable ability to fell trees and shrubs not only impacts the physical structure of the forest, but also creates open spaces beneficial to a variety of other species.

This unique ability to modify their environment not only represents an adaptation to their nomadic lifestyle, but also a vital ecological service that contributes to the dynamic configuration and overall health of the landscapes they call home.

The influence of elephants on forest structure is evident in the way they manipulate and fell trees of different sizes.

This behavior not only alters the architecture of the forest, but also generates clearings and open spaces, enriching the diversity of habitats available in the ecosystem. These open spaces become favorable areas for the growth of herbs and shorter plants, creating ecological niches that benefit various species of animals, from smaller herbivores to birds and insects.

The ability of elephants to actively modify their environment not only has local consequences, but also has an impact at the landscape level.

The open spaces created by their activity, known as elephant glades, not only promote biodiversity, but can also influence patterns of forest regeneration and, therefore, the long-term structure of landscapes. This process of active modification of the environment by elephants contributes to an ecological dynamic that goes beyond their role as simple consumers of vegetation.

The active participation of elephants in ecological succession is presented as a fundamental component for the evolution and continued health of the ecosystems they inhabit.

As these majestic herbivores consume vegetation and alter their environment, they have a significant impact on the dynamics of landscapes, making way for new plants and facilitating changes in ecosystem structure.

This dynamic process, which extends beyond simply being an adaptive strategy for their survival, becomes a crucial element for the resistance and resilience of the habitats they share with other species.

The role of elephants in ecological succession is especially notable in their ability to transform the landscape through their herbivorous activity and their unique ability to fell trees and shrubs.

By selectively consuming vegetation, they create opportunities for natural regeneration and new plant growth. Additionally, by felling trees, they create clearings and open spaces that encourage habitat diversity, creating beneficial ecological niches for a variety of species, from insects to smaller mammals.

This dynamic process of ecological succession is not only beneficial for local biodiversity, but also contributes to the adaptation and resilience of ecosystems.

Elephants' ability to reshape their environment not only creates favorable conditions for the survival of diverse species, but also establishes a cycle of regeneration that strengthens the overall health of the habitat. In a world where ecosystems face constant challenges, elephants' active participation in ecological succession highlights the importance of their role as inadvertent architects of the landscape.

This dynamic process is not only an adaptive evolutionary strategy for elephants, but also an invaluable ecological service that contributes to the stability and sustainability of ecosystems.

The conservation of elephants, which often face significant threats, is not only essential to ensure their survival, but also to maintain the vitality and functionality of the habitats they inhabit. Ultimately, elephants' participation in ecological succession highlights the critical need to preserve and protect these animals as active and fundamental guardians of the health of our ecosystems

Despite their vital role in ecology, coexistence between elephants and human communities presents significant challenges that must be addressed with care and effective strategies.
.

Competition for resources, especially in regions where living space is reduced due to human expansion, can lead to conflicts between these majestic mammals and local communities. In this context, careful management and conservation strategies that seek a balance between the needs of elephants and those of human communities become crucial elements to achieve harmonious and sustainable coexistence.

The expansion of human settlements and the transformation of natural habitat can lead to a decrease in the spaces available for elephants, which in turn intensifies competition for water, food and space. This competition can trigger conflicts, such as the destruction of agricultural crops by elephants in search of food, which in turn creates tensions between the animals and local communities.

The careful management of this interaction between elephants and human communities is essential to prevent and mitigate conflicts.

Strategies that involve the delimitation of protected areas, the implementation of conflict prevention measures, and the education of both local communities and wildlife guardians are key elements in this management approach.

The consideration of the needs and natural behaviors of elephants, as well as the understanding of practices and ways of life of human communities, contribute to developing more effective and sustainable strategies.

In addition, conservation strategies must seek not only the protection of elephants, but also the welfare and security of human communities.

The promotion of sustainable agricultural practices, the development of innovative solutions for conflict mitigation, and the implementation of educational programs that promote harmonious coexistence are crucial aspects of an integral conservation approach.

The conservation of elephants goes beyond the mere preservation of a species; it implies the salvaguardia de la riqueza y complicitas de los ecosistemas que comparten.

The existence of elephants in a natural environment is not only a testament to their incredible adaptation and evolution over time, but also reflects the vital interconnection between these majestic animals and the overall health of their habitats.

In this sense, strategies that promote harmonious coexistence between humans and elephants become imperative to maintain ecological balance and ensure a sustainable future for both parties.

Harmonious coexistence between humans and elephants requires a comprehensive approach that encompasses various dimensions. Education is presented as a fundamental pillar, since it promotes awareness and understanding of the importance of elephants in the ecosystem, as well as the measures necessary to minimize conflicts between local communities and these animals. Conservation awareness not only promotes valuing wildlife, but also encourages sustainable practices that benefit both humans and elephants.

Collaboration between local communities and scientists not only enriches the knowledge base, but also promotes the active participation of people in conservation. The involvement of communities in decision-making and implementation of conservation strategies ensures a comprehensive perspective that addresses the needs of both humans and elephants.

This dance, woven from the inextricable interaction between these majestic animals and their environment, reveals an intriguing picture of how elephants are not only consumers, but also unwitting architects of the landscapes they inhabit.

In our next chapter, we will unravel the intimate facet of reproduction and family dynamics of these extraordinary beings. We will delve into the emotional bonds, complex family hierarchies and mating rituals that define the intimate lives of elephants.

In doing so, we will unveil a deeply moving and revealing aspect of their existence, revealing how these terrestrial giants are not only essential to the health of ecosystems, but also to the continuity and richness of their own species.

Chapter 6
Reproduction and Family Dynamics

Reproduction among elephants, far from being simply a biological act intended for the perpetuation of the species, is revealed as a complex emotional dance between mothers and calves, marked by a moving depth in family relationships.

This connection, particularly between a mother elephant and her calf, goes beyond mere reproductive function; It is an unbreakable bond that defines the very essence of the family unit in the kingdom of these majestic animals.

The exceptional dedication of mother elephants to their calves is a moving testament to the complexity and richness of family relationships in the world of these terrestrial giants.

In this emotional ballet, mothers display a devotion that transcends the limits of instinct, offering care and protection with a dedication that highlights the depth of their family ties. This exceptional maternal behavior not only guarantees the survival of the calf, but also reveals an emotional dimension in the lives of elephants that awakens the empathy and admiration of those who observe these touching family exchanges.

The relationship between a mother elephant and her calf manifests itself in a series of fascinating behaviors. The mother, in her protective role, guides and teaches her young the intricacies of life in the pack.

We watch as the mother shares wisdom, from identifying food sources to navigating complex territories. The calf, in turn, responds with a palpable emotional connection, following in its mother's footsteps and seeking comfort and security in her presence.

This act of maternal care not only occurs during the first years of the calf's life, but persists over time, even when the calf grows and becomes independent.

Elephant mothers continue to play an active role in protecting and guiding their calves, evidencing a long-term dedication that transcends the initial phases of childhood. This long relationship and family cohesion underscore the importance of family relationships in the social structure of elephants, contributing to the strength and stability of the herd as a whole.

The fascinating family dynamics of elephants unfold in a narrative that goes beyond the relationship between mother and calf, extending to integrate into a herd that emerges as a solid and complex social nucleus.

These packs, composed primarily of related females and their offspring, reveal an intricate web of relationships that transcends mere biology, creating an environment in which support and protection are fundamentally intertwined.

This social system not only provides a structure of security, but also serves as a platform for continuous learning and transmission of knowledge across generations.

Dentro de la manada, cada miembro desempeña un papel crucial en la cohesión y funcionamiento del grupo. Las hembras relacionadas, lideradas por una matriarca experimentada, colaboran de manera armoniosa en la crianza y protección de las crías. Este sistema de apoyo entre parientes crea una red de seguridad que se extiende más allá de la relación madre-hija, abarcando tías, primas y hermanas.

Esta compleja estructura social no solo fortalece los lazos familiares, sino que también refleja la importancia de la colaboración y la interdependencia en la supervivencia de la manada.

La manada, además de brindar seguridad física, actúa como un entorno de aprendizaje vital para las crías. Los jóvenes elefantes observan y participan en interacciones sociales, aprendiendo habilidades esenciales para la vida, desde la identificación de fuentes de alimentos hasta la navegación en su entorno.

Este proceso de aprendizaje no solo ocurre a través de la observación, sino que también implica una enseñanza activa por parte de las hembras más experimentadas, que comparten sus conocimientos acumulados.

The transmission of knowledge within the herd is a continuous and essential phenomenon for the survival and adaptability of the species. Shared experiences and wisdom accumulated over generations become an invaluable treasure, contributing to the herd's resilience and ability to adapt to changing environmental challenges. The pack, therefore, not only serves as an emotional support system, but also functions as a living library of practical knowledge that is carefully passed down from one generation to the next.

Within the intricate fabric of the pack, each member performs defined roles and responsibilities, contributing to the harmony and functionality of the group. Older females, imbued with invaluable experience accumulated over the years, often emerge as natural leaders, taking on the responsibility of guiding and directing the pack.

This maternal leadership becomes a fundamental pillar for social cohesion and decision-making in the group, since these matriarchs not only provide guidance in the search for resources and protection, but also share their wisdom in parenting.

Although males tend to be more solitary in their behavior, their role within the pack is equally crucial and multifaceted. During the mating season, males play an active role in searching for mates and competing for the favor of females in heat.

This period, full of intricate interactions and courtship rituals, highlights the importance of the contribution of males in ensuring the continuity of the species. Furthermore, beyond this specific season, males also play a prominent role in protecting the herd against possible external threats, showing a protective instinct and a willingness to face challenges for the benefit of the group.

The collaboration and coordination between the different members of the pack create a dynamic balance that favors the survival and prosperity of the whole. The complex interactions and relationships between elephants within the herd reflect a structured society where each individual, regardless of gender, contributes significantly to the collective well-being.

In addition to primary roles, the herd also provides an environment conducive to the development of social and cognitive skills, especially in young elephants.

These younger members learn not only from their mothers, aunts, and sisters, but also from interaction with other members of the pack. This social learning dynamic contributes to the comprehensive development of the offspring, preparing them to face the challenges of the environment more effectively.

The richness of family relationships among elephants is not limited solely to closeness with parents and siblings; extends to forming strong bonds with elephant uncles and aunts.

This extensive, intricate and emotional family structure goes beyond direct relationships, contributing not only to social cohesion within the pack, but also providing an additional support system for the offspring. In this relational network, the network of caregivers and mentors expands, enriching the growth and development experience of new generations of elephants.

The importance of uncles and aunts in the lives of baby elephants is evident in the variety of roles they play. They not only become additional sources of guidance and care, but also actively participate in the transmission of knowledge and skills essential for survival in the environment.

The experience accumulated by these more experienced members of the pack becomes a valuable resource for the cubs, as they learn not only from the teachings of their mothers, but also from the wisdom shared by uncles and aunts.

The extended family structure of elephants, which includes relationships with uncles and aunts, creates a support network that is not only limited to immediate nurturing and protection, but also extends over time.

This continuous support system is essential for the well-being and adaptability of the pups, allowing them to safely explore their environment and learn the intricacies of life in the pack. Furthermore, the presence of uncles and aunts further strengthens family ties, fostering collaboration and solidarity within the group.

This extended family environment also plays a crucial role in the socialization of baby elephants. Interaction with uncles and aunts provides calves the opportunity to develop social skills, learn hierarchies within the pack, and understand the dynamics of complex social interactions. This socialization process is essential for the comprehensive development of the offspring and their successful integration into the social structure of the pack.

Herd life for elephants not only represents a complex social group, but also an environment enriched with countless learning opportunities that are essential for the comprehensive development of the offspring.

In this dynamic social fabric, calves are not only witnesses but also active participants in social rituals and behaviors that define the communication and norms of elephant society. These rituals, rich in complexity and subtlety, are not only essential for the individual survival of each elephant, but also play a critical role in the ability of the entire herd to successfully adapt to its environment.

Observation and participation of the young in these social rituals provide them with a practical and valuable education about the complexities of life in society. From interactions between adult members to games between offspring, each moment contributes to the development of social skills, the understanding of hierarchies and the acquisition of the norms that govern life in the pack.

This learning process, guided by immersion in the daily life of the pack, allows the calves to not only acquire fundamental skills, but also develop a deep understanding of the culture and social dynamics of their species.

Elephant social rituals encompass a wide range of behaviors, from moments of play that strengthen social bonds to complex vocalizations that serve as a sophisticated means of communication. By participating in these rituals, the pups not only hone their motor and cognitive skills, but also learn to interpret key social cues, such as facial expressions, body gestures, and vocalizations.

The importance of these rituals lies not only in individual survival, but also in the adaptation and continued success of the pack in its environment.

The ability to communicate effectively, understand social dynamics, and respond collectively to environmental challenges are key elements to the long-term survival and prosperity of the herd. Rituals, being an integral part of daily life, contribute to social cohesion and the development of social intelligence of elephants, crucial aspects for adaptability and resistance to changes in the environment.

Communication between elephants is presented as a fascinating expression of sophistication and diversity in the animal kingdom. Through an amalgamation of sounds, gestures and tactile vibrations transmitted through their corpulent bodies, these majestic animals not only communicate functionally, but also establish complex emotional connections within the herd.

This intricate network of communication is revealed as a subtle and multifaceted language that significantly strengthens social bonds.

Sound communication between elephants encompasses a wide range of vocalizations, from resonant trumpets to deep roars that are imperceptible to the human ear.

These sounds not only serve as means of transmitting information about the location of resources, the presence of predators, or environmental conditions, but they also express a rich palette of emotions. Elephants use these sounds to share joy, express anxieties and communicate moods, thus forming an emotional language that goes beyond mere communicative functionality.

In addition to vocal communication, elephants use a variety of physical gestures that enrich their ability to express themselves.

Ear movements, specific body postures and facial gestures are used to convey subtle messages about intentions, emotions and alertness. These gestures, which are an integral part of elephant-elephant communication, reinforce social bonds by allowing a deeper understanding of emotional dynamics and individual intentions within the herd.

A particularly notable facet of communication between elephants is the use of tactile vibrations through their bodies. Through their ability to detect vibrations through their legs and bodies, elephants can communicate over considerably long distances, which is essential for coordinating actions and warning of potential dangers.

This form of tactile communication contributes not only to the effectiveness of interaction within the pack, but also to the building of close relationships based on trust and cooperation.

This intricate communication network between elephants therefore becomes a crucial element for the social cohesion of the herd.

By providing a means to share information, express emotions, and coordinate actions, this complex network of communicative signals contributes to the formation and maintenance of social structure. Deep understanding of these communication systems highlights not only the exceptional social intelligence of elephants, but also the richness of their emotional and social lives.

The reproduction and family dynamics of elephants stand as the common thread that weaves the continuous life cycle of these majestic animals. From tender childhood to the wisdom of old age, each stage of life contributes uniquely to the pack's rich collective narrative.

The childhood of elephants, marked by curiosity and exploration, is revealed as a vital chapter where the calves absorb the teachings of their mothers, aunts and uncles, preparing to face the challenges of adult life.

As we move into adulthood, we see how social dynamics intertwine in a complex ballet, where mother-child relationships, peer alliances, and interactions with herd leaders define the structure and stability of the elephant community.

In the advanced stages of life, old age brings with it a wealth of experiences and accumulated wisdom, with older elephants playing a vital role as guardians of the herd's collective memory.

Guardians of herd life, from conservationists to scientists to local communities, are coming together in a collective effort to safeguard the future of these terrestrial giants. In this exciting chapter, we will delve into stories of dedication, innovation, and bravery, revealing how humanity strives to be co-stewards of this epicenter of animal life.

The next chapter will immerse us in the challenges that this life cycle faces: the constant pressure on the habitat, the threat of poaching and the growing conflicts with human communities. We will explore how conservation efforts have become beacons of hope, seeking not only to protect elephants, but also to preserve the delicate balance of their family relationships.

Chapter 7
Conservation Challenges and Efforts

In this chapter, we will confront the challenges that threaten the existence of elephants and explore the crucial conservation efforts that seek to protect these majestic giants. Poaching pressure, habitat loss and human-elephant conflict are just some of the challenges they face, and overcoming them requires a global commitment to preserve the elephants' legacy for generations to come.

One of the most pressing and devastating challenges facing elephants today is poaching for ivory. Throughout history, elephant tusks have been desired due to their beauty and value, leading to indiscriminate hunting practices and an alarming decline in elephant populations.

The illegal ivory trade has emerged as a constant and pernicious threat to the survival of these majestic animals.

This scourge dates back to times past, when the beauty and rarity of ivory led to demand for this material skyrocketing. Poaching, fueled by this demand, has put undue pressure on elephant populations around the world. The shocking image of elephants stripped of their tusks has tragically become a symbol of the struggle these animals face at the hands of human greed.

The decline in elephant populations not only affects numbers, but also has a profound impact on the social structure and family dynamics of the herds.

The loss of adult individuals, especially those with crucial experiences and roles, leaves a void that resonates throughout the elephant community. Furthermore, the calves, deprived of the guidance and protection of more experienced elephants, face even greater challenges.

Poaching/Hunting has led to elephant conservation not being simply an altruistic act, but an urgent need to preserve biodiversity and maintain ecological balance in the ecosystems they inhabit. Declining elephant populations can have cascading effects on ecosystems, affecting seed dispersal, landscape structure, and interactions with other species.

Fortunately, global awareness of this issue has led to significant conservation efforts and campaigns against the illegal ivory trade. Organizations, governments and activists have come together to implement stricter anti-poaching measures, promote the protection of critical habitats and raise awareness about the importance of elephant conservation.

Human expansion and voracious demand for natural resources have triggered significant habitat loss for elephants, marking a dark chapter in the coexistence between humanity and these majestic animals.

Human encroachment, driven by the expansion of urban areas, intensive agriculture and resource extraction, has transformed the landscapes that elephants have called home since time immemorial.

The fragmentation and destruction of their natural habitats have created insurmountable barriers to the movement of the herds, limiting their access to areas crucial for food, water and other essential resources. This habitat loss not only intensifies competition for resources among elephants, but also increases the vulnerability of these populations to external threats, such as poaching and conflicts with human communities.

Effective elephant conservation cannot be limited to simply protecting individuals; must comprehensively address the preservation and, where necessary, the restoration of critical habitats.

The recovery of degraded areas and the connection of ecological corridors are fundamental strategies to restore the mobility of herds and guarantee the long-term viability of these populations.

Protecting critical habitats involves not only the creation of reserves and protected areas, but also the implementation of sustainable practices in surrounding areas that allow harmonious coexistence between elephants and human communities. Environmental education and the active participation of local communities are essential to forge a sustainable balance between the needs of both, ensuring peaceful coexistence and the preservation of these vital environments.

As shared spaces between elephants and human communities decrease, the increasing intersection between these two worlds has led to a significant increase in conflicts.

Competition for resources, especially in regions where living space is limited, has led to increasingly frequent and, in some cases, dangerous encounters between elephants and humans. This phenomenon, marked by tensions and challenges, raises crucial questions about the peaceful and sustainable coexistence between these two species in a shared environment.

The expansion of urban areas, intensive agriculture and the fragmentation of natural habitats have reduced the territories available for both elephants and human communities. In this scenario of competition for resources, encounters between elephants and humans have become inevitable, generating conflicts that can put the safety and well-being of both parties at risk.

Careful management of these conflicts becomes essential to address the complex dynamics between elephants and human communities. Coexistence strategies must be implemented in a comprehensive manner, taking into consideration the needs and natural behaviors of both. This involves not only protecting critical areas for food and water access, but also implementing preventive measures to avoid unwanted encounters.

Electric fences, early warnings and sustainable agricultural practices are valuable tools in conflict management. These measures not only protect crops and human property, but also contribute to the safety of elephants by avoiding stressful and potentially dangerous situations.

Educating local communities about elephant behavior and coexistence strategies also plays a crucial role in reducing misunderstandings and promoting harmonious coexistence.

Fortunately, amid these monumental challenges, a united front of conservation efforts aimed at protecting and preserving elephants has emerged. This global movement, driven by the urgency to counter poaching, mitigate habitat loss, and establish strategies to foster peaceful coexistence between human communities and these majestic giants, reflects the dedication and collaboration of various entities.

International organizations, such as the World Wildlife Fund (WWF) and the International Union for Conservation of Nature (IUCN), have played a key role in raising global awareness, raising funds and implementing concrete projects to combat poaching and protect wildlife. critical elephant habitats.

These large-scale efforts have helped establish a network of protected areas and ecological corridors, creating safe havens for the herds.

At the government level, many countries have strengthened their laws and policies to combat poaching and protect elephants. Implementing sustainable habitat management strategies and promoting wildlife-friendly agricultural practices are crucial steps in the direction of harmonious coexistence between elephants and human communities.

Local communities also play a central role in these conservation efforts. Environmental education programs, economic empowerment and active community participation are key elements to foster mutual understanding and build bridges towards peaceful coexistence. When communities become allies in protecting elephants, it creates a strong foundation for long-term conservation.

The battle against poaching has triggered the implementation of intensive security programs designed to protect elephants from deadly threats. The increasing sophistication of the methods used by poachers to obtain the precious tusks of these animals has led to the formation of specialized patrols equipped with the latest monitoring technologies.

This comprehensive approach seeks not only to protect elephants, but also to actively deter and confront those who seek to inflict harm on these majestic beings.

Specialized patrols, made up of highly trained teams committed to protecting wildlife, play a crucial role in the defense of elephants. These units patrol critical areas, implementing preventative strategies and acting proactively to intercept and stop any poaching attempts. Their visible presence and expert knowledge not only create a deterrent, but also constitute an active line of defense against threats to elephants' lives.

The incorporation of advanced monitoring technologies adds a cutting-edge component to these conservation efforts. Satellite tracking systems, infrared cameras and acoustic sensors combine to provide constant surveillance of critical areas, allowing a rapid and coordinated response to any suspicious activity.

This technological infrastructure not only improves the effectiveness of patrols, but also generates valuable data that contributes to the understanding of elephant movement patterns and behavior, thereby informing more effective conservation strategies.

International collaboration plays a vital role in this fight, as poaching is a cross-border phenomenon. Coordinated efforts between countries, international organizations and NGOs strengthen global response capacity, sharing information, resources and best practices. This unified approach not only amplifies the effectiveness of security measures, but also contributes to building a global protection network for elephants.

The protection and restoration of critical elephant habitats emerge as essential pillars in the fight to ensure the long-term survival of these majestic creatures.

In a world where human expansion and degradation of the natural environment have led to the decline of wildlife territories, efforts aimed at preserving and revitalizing habitats have become imperative.

Innovative programs that engage local communities in sustainable land management have proven to be effective tools for creating a harmonious balance between human needs and environmental preservation.

These programs not only recognize the importance of active community participation in decision-making related to natural resource management, but also foster a sense of shared responsibility towards the conservation of elephant habitat.

Promoting ecotourism is another valuable strategy in protecting elephant habitats. By encouraging sustainable tourism practices that respect local ecosystems and generate income for communities, ecotourism becomes a powerful tool to preserve and restore crucial habitats.

Additionally, well-managed ecotourism can serve as a source of environmental awareness, educating visitors about the importance of conservation and respectful coexistence with wildlife.

Habitat restoration is not only about reversing environmental degradation, but also about strengthening the resilience of ecosystems. Reforestation projects, rehabilitation of degraded areas and the creation of ecological corridors are specific measures that seek to restore the functionality and vitality of elephant habitats.

Doing so not only benefits the lives of these majestic animals, but also contributes to the overall well-being of biodiversity and the health of surrounding ecosystems.

Education and awareness, as key elements in conservation efforts, play a crucial role in building bridges between human communities and elephants.

Programs designed to inform and educate local communities about the fundamental importance of elephants in ecosystems and their intrinsic value not only generate deeper understanding, but also contribute to establishing a solid foundation for harmonious coexistence.

Environmental education not only focuses on transmitting knowledge about the biology, behavior and ecological role of elephants, but also highlights the interdependence between the health of these terrestrial giants and the general well-being of ecosystems. By understanding how elephant preservation contributes to biodiversity and natural balance, local communities can appreciate the critical importance of protecting and coexisting with these majestic animals.

Awareness programs seek to go beyond purely academic education, seeking to generate empathy and emotional connection between people and elephants.

By highlighting the individual stories, the challenges these creatures face, and their unique contributions to ecology, a sense of responsibility and care for their well-being is fostered. This emotional connection is essential to inspire positive actions and promote daily practices that promote respectful coexistence with elephants.

Furthermore, education and awareness can act as catalysts for the active participation of communities in conservation projects. By understanding the direct impact of their actions on the preservation of elephant habitats and safety, communities can become valuable allies in the fight for conservation.

Preserving the legacy of elephants goes beyond simply protecting a species; It is a commitment to safeguarding the cultural, ecological and historical wealth that these majestic beings represent in the diverse ecosystems they call home. These land giants, with their imposing presence and vital role in the history and mythology of many cultures, have forged a unique connection with humans over the centuries.

The relationship between humans and elephants has deep roots in the history, mythology and spirituality of various communities. These creatures have been revered, depicted in works of art, and have played significant roles in cultural narratives.

CHAPTER 8
HUMAN-ELEPHANT CONFLICT AND COEXISTENCE

In this chapter, we will explore the complex and sometimes challenging world of human-elephant interaction. As habitats overlap and resources become scarcer, conflict arises that requires deep understanding and innovative solutions. Through this exploration, we will seek ways to foster peaceful and sustainable coexistence between two seemingly divergent worlds.

As human communities experience continued growth and the boundaries of natural habitats are compromised, an intricate interweaving develops between the worlds of elephants and humans.

79

This crossing of paths gives rise to conflict situations, where competition for essential resources, such as water and food, intensifies, creating a significant challenge for the harmonious coexistence between both species.

Increasing demand for land for urban expansion, agriculture and other human activities has led to an inevitable reduction in elephants' natural habitats.

This process of habitat fragmentation not only limits the territories available to elephants, but also forces them to enter areas inhabited by humans in search of resources critical to their survival. In this border crossing, inevitable competition arises that often triggers conflicts between both species.

Competition for resources manifests itself in various ways, from the search for water to obtaining food in agricultural areas.

The pressure on these resources is especially evident in regions where living space is reduced, generating tensions that affect both human communities and elephants.

These conflicts not only pose a threat to the security and well-being of both sides, but also pose considerable challenges to the conservation of elephants in the wild.

Human-elephant conflict, an increasingly prominent challenge in the conservation landscape, has deep roots in competition for limited resources.

The growing expansion of human populations, accompanied by the transformation of land for agriculture and urban development, has significantly altered natural landscapes, pushing elephants out of their natural habitats in search of food. This change in elephant movement and migration patterns has increased the chances of conflictive encounters with human communities.

Increasing demand for land for agriculture, urbanization and other human activities has led to the fragmentation and reduction of elephants' natural habitats.

Relying on vast expanses of land to meet their dietary needs, these magnificent animals are forced to adapt to a changing environment, often entering human-inhabited areas in their constant search for essential resources.

This phenomenon of intrusion into human territories generates conflict situations, since both humans and elephants compete for critical resources such as water and vegetation. Elephants, in their need to find food, can damage crops and property, causing tensions with local communities that depend on agriculture for their livelihood.

The increased frequency of confrontational encounters not only poses threats to the safety and well-being of both parties, but also represents a significant challenge to conservation efforts.

Peaceful coexistence between humans and elephants becomes essential for the preservation of these animals and the promotion of biodiversity in general.

One of the main points of friction in the human-elephant conflict lies in the incursion of elephants into agricultural areas. This phenomenon, often referred to as "crop conflict," has become a constant source of concern for local communities. The destruction of crops and property by elephants not only represents a direct threat to the food and economic security of communities, but also intensifies tensions and aggravates conflict between both species.

The incursion of elephants into agricultural fields can have devastating consequences for local farmers, who depend on their crops for their livelihood. Crop loss due to the presence of elephants can translate into significant economic impacts and increase the vulnerability of communities already facing socioeconomic challenges.

In addition to economic losses, the destruction of crops also generates emotional and social tensions in communities. The frustration and fear associated with the possibility of conflictual encounters with elephants can affect the quality of life and psychological well-being of people living in these areas.

Effectively addressing this flashpoint requires integrated approaches that consider both the conservation needs of elephants and the interests and security of local communities. Strategies ranging from mitigation measures, such as protective fencing and early warning systems, to the promotion of sustainable agricultural practices and compensation for losses, have been implemented in various locations to reduce tensions and foster coexistence.

Close encounters between elephants and humans, while fascinating and full of potential for mutual understanding, also present significant risks to the safety of both species. Elephants, highly intelligent and emotional beings, can feel threatened in certain situations and react defensively, which, unfortunately, can endanger people's lives. Understanding and mitigating these risks becomes an essential task to promote safe and harmonious coexistence.

The defensive reaction of elephants can manifest itself in various ways, from mock charges to more aggressive behaviors in situations of stress or perceived threat.

Additionally, awareness and respect for wildlife are critical components of promoting safe coexistence. Public education about elephant behavior and needs can reduce conflictive encounters and encourage more respectful and safe coexistence.

Despite persistent challenges, the search for innovative strategies to foster peaceful coexistence between elephants and human communities is underway. Efforts are focused on implementing practical and sustainable solutions that address the fundamental problems of human-elephant conflict. Among these strategies, physical barriers and advanced monitoring technologies stand out, which are playing an essential role in mitigating risks and promoting safety for both species.

Crop protection fences have become a valuable tool in minimizing elephant incursion into agricultural areas. These physical barriers, designed specifically to protect crops, not only act as an effective line of defense, but also enable coexistence by reducing the potential for property damage.

Advanced monitoring technologies have revolutionized human-elephant conflict management. Early warning systems based on sensors and cameras can detect the presence of elephants in nearby areas and send notifications to communities, giving them the time necessary to take preventive measures. These technological solutions not only improve safety, but also enable more efficient and sustainable management of human-elephant encounters.

The use of drones and satellite tracking systems has also gained popularity as monitoring tools, providing real-time information on elephant movements and helping to anticipate potential conflictive interactions. These technological innovations contribute not only to safety, but also to a deeper understanding of elephant behavioral patterns, facilitating more informed conservation approaches.

Creating wildlife corridors and promoting connectivity between natural habitats emerge as crucial approaches in managing human-elephant conflict.

These corridors are not only a vital tool for elephant conservation, but also play an essential role in promoting harmonious coexistence between these majestic creatures and human communities.

Wildlife corridors are strategically planned strips of land that allow elephants to move from one area to another safely and without human interference. These corridors, carefully designed to connect fragmented habitats, offer alternative routes for elephants, thus avoiding incursion into densely populated areas and significantly reducing conflict encounters.

Promoting connectivity between natural habitats through the creation of corridors not only benefits elephants, but also contributes to the preservation of biodiversity in general.

These corridors not only facilitate the migratory movements of elephants, but also allow other species to share and maintain natural movement patterns, thus strengthening local ecosystems.

Planning and establishing wildlife corridors requires comprehensive collaboration between governments, local communities and conservation organizations. Collective efforts to identify and protect critical migration routes help ensure that elephants have access to feeding, water and breeding areas essential to their survival, while minimizing conflictive interactions with human communities.

Education and awareness emerge as fundamental pillars in the management of human-elephant conflict, playing a crucial role in building bridges of understanding and coexistence. By informing communities about elephant behavior, safety measures and the importance of coexistence, a framework is established that fosters mutual understanding and cultivates positive attitudes towards wildlife.

The education not only imparts knowledge about elephant biology and behavior, but also highlights the critical importance of preserving these majestic animals and their habitats.

Awareness-raising also plays an essential role in advocating for the adoption of appropriate security measures. Through awareness campaigns, crucial information can be conveyed on how to behave in the presence of elephants, including preventive measures and the importance of maintaining a safe distance. This not only protects human communities but also safeguards the safety and well-being of the elephants themselves.

In addition, raising awareness contributes to forging a sense of shared responsibility in conservation. By recognizing the importance of coexistence and how individual actions can have a positive impact on wildlife preservation, communities can become active advocates for the protection of elephants and biodiversity in general.

Managing human-elephant conflict is not limited to short-term solutions; rather, it requires long-term strategies that address the root causes of conflict and establish a sustainable balance between the needs of both species.

Estas estrategias, que se centran en la planificación del uso de la tierra y la promoción de prácticas agrícolas sostenibles, son fundamentales para garantizar una convivencia armoniosa y equitativa en el futuro.

La planificación del uso de la tierra emerge como un componente crucial en la gestión a largo plazo del conflicto. En muchos casos, la expansión humana ha llevado a la transformación de hábitats naturales en áreas agrícolas o urbanas, creando tensiones y conflictos entre elefantes y comunidades locales.

Estrategias que consideran cuidadosamente la zonificación del uso del suelo, identificando y protegiendo áreas críticas para los elefantes, contribuyen a minimizar la pérdida de hábitat y a prevenir encuentros conflictivos.

La promoción de prácticas agrícolas sostenibles es otra piedra angular en la gestión a largo plazo. Al adoptar enfoques agrícolas que minimizan el impacto en los hábitats naturales, las comunidades pueden reducir la atracción de los elefantes hacia las áreas agrícolas.

CHAPTER 9
CAPTIVITY AND ETHICAL CONSIDERATIONS

Zoos, throughout history, have been meeting points where the public can marvel and admire the diversity of wildlife. However, the captivity of elephants in these specific environments has raised growing ethical concerns and deep reflections on the well-being of these majestic animals.

While it is undeniable that some zoos strive to provide conditions that mimic elephants' natural habitat, the reality of limited space and, in some cases, lack of meaningful enrichment pose challenges that can negatively impact the mental and physical health of these giants. of the nature.

This ethical dilemma has led to a change in the perception and approach of many zoos, with an increase in awareness of the need to address ethical concerns.

The ethical questioning surrounding the captivity of elephants in zoos focuses on the capacity of these closed environments to offer a full and satisfactory life to animals that, in their natural habitat, have large territories of movement and a complex social structure.

Although some zoos have implemented measures to improve conditions, such as expanded habitats and enrichment programs, fundamental challenges remain related to adapting these animals to an environment that is, by definition, restrictive.

Space limitation is one of the most obvious challenges. Although some zoos have adopted larger, more naturalistic habitat designs, the ability to provide the same range of movement and experiences they would have in the wild remains a challenge intrinsic to captivity.

Additionally, a lack of environmental enrichment, such as foraging and complex social interaction, can result in an impoverished environment for elephants, affecting both their physical and emotional well-being.

Some zoos are looking for new ways to balance their educational and conservation role with respect for animal welfare, taking steps to increase the quality of life for captive elephants.

Sanctuaries, in stark contrast to zoos, have emerged as refuges intended to provide an environment closer to nature and focused exclusively on the well-being of elephants.

These sanctuaries often serve as places of retreat and rehabilitation for animals rescued from precarious situations, seeking to provide them with an environment in which they can recover physically and emotionally. However, even in these environments that seek to be ethical refuges, ethical questions remain, as elephants may face challenges related to adapting to their new life and managing social interactions.

Unlike zoos, sanctuaries strive to recreate environments that more closely mimic elephants' natural conditions. This involves providing large and varied areas for movement, as well as opportunities for the expression of natural behaviors, such as foraging and complex social interaction.

Sanctuaries often take a more holistic approach to animal welfare, prioritizing the physical and emotional health of elephants over public entertainment considerations.

However, even in these ethical environments, questions and challenges arise. Adapting elephants to a new environment can be a complex process that requires time and patience. Additionally, managing social interactions between rescued elephants, which often come from different traumatic situations, can present unique challenges.

Reintegrating elephants into healthy social groups is a critical aspect of sanctuary work and highlights the importance of understanding and addressing the complexities of these animals' social dynamics.

Ethical considerations in elephant captivity encompass a wide range of issues, each raising profound questions about the relationship between humans and elephants in controlled environments.

 From the physical conditions in which elephants are kept to the nature of their interaction with the public, constant evaluation of these issues has become essential to ensure that captivity practices are aligned with the highest ethical standards and are prioritized. in animal welfare.

In terms of physical conditions, the space available for elephants in captivity is a critical factor. Limited space can negatively affect your natural behavior, physical health, and emotional well-being. Constantly evaluating the suitability of habitats and finding ways to improve and expand these environments are essential ethical considerations.

Additionally, providing environmental stimulation and opportunities for the expression of natural behaviors, such as foraging and social interaction, are key components to ensuring quality of life for captive elephants.

Interaction with the public also raises significant ethical questions. Elephants in captivity are often displayed for human entertainment, whether in zoos, circuses, or other venues. Ethical evaluation of these interactions involves considering the potential impact on the emotional well-being of the elephants, as well as the ethics of using these animals for human enjoyment.

Questions about the naturalness and authenticity of the activities carried out in these contexts also come into play, and it is essential to seek a balance that respects the integrity and dignity of elephants.

Continued review and adjustment of captivity practices are therefore imperative to address these complex ethical considerations. Ethical standards evolve over time as a deeper understanding of the needs and behaviors of elephants is gained, and the constant adaptation of captivity practices reflects a commitment to the well-being of these majestic animals.

The physical and mental health of captive elephants is at the center of ethical and animal welfare concerns.

Adequate veterinary care is a fundamental pillar in the care of captive elephants. Regular check-ups, attention to dental health, monitoring of reproductive health and timely treatment of any medical problems are essential to ensure elephants receive the level of care they deserve.

Environmental enrichment is another key tool to promote the physical and mental health of captive elephants. Providing elements such as climbing structures, interactive toys, and foraging opportunities recreates conditions closer to their natural habitat, stimulating their mind and encouraging natural behaviors.

Furthermore, this enrichment not only prevents boredom, but also helps reduce stress and improve the quality of life of captive elephants.

In terms of physical health, space allocation is essential. A large, naturalistic habitat allows elephants to exercise their muscles and satisfy their inherent need to move over long distances.

This not only supports your physical well-being, but also helps prevent health problems related to inactivity and lack of exercise. This proactive approach to veterinary care helps address health problems before they become critical situations.

Cognitive and social stimulation also play a crucial role in the mental well-being of elephants. Creating opportunities for social interaction between elephants, especially for those who have been rescued from precarious situations, encourages the formation of bonds and the reconstruction of the natural social dynamics of these animals. Introducing cognitive challenges, such as food puzzles and games, helps keep elephants' minds active, contributing to their mental well-being over time.

Interacting with the public in elephant captivity settings not only raises fundamental ethical questions, but also highlights the need to address these challenges in a thoughtful and balanced manner.

While education can be a powerful tool to raise conservation awareness and highlight the importance of elephant preservation, this educational process must be carefully managed to find the right balance.

Educating the public about elephant conservation and the protection of their habitat is essential to foster awareness and action on behalf of these species. However, it is imperative to find ways to conduct this education in an ethical and respectful manner.

Strategies that minimize stress for elephants and allow them to make autonomous choices are essential. This could include implementing time limits for interaction with the public, as well as creating environments that allow elephants to retreat to quieter areas when they wish.

Consideration of elephants' capacity for choice and autonomy is crucial. Elephants are intelligent and social beings, and their well-being is influenced by the way interactions with the public are handled.

Allowing elephants the option to participate or withdraw from interactive activities provides a more ethical and respectful approach towards these animals.

Furthermore, constant evaluation of methods of interaction with the public is essential to ensure that they are aligned with the highest ethical standards. This involves careful monitoring of individual elephant responses and continuous adaptation of practices based on the animals' needs and preferences.

The ethical question in conservation becomes a crucial thread when addressing decisions related to the captivity of species, and this dynamic becomes more complex when it comes to the preservation of elephants.

The fundamental question of whether the preservation of a species justifies its confinement in captivity is a hot topic that requires careful and balanced exploration. In this context, ethics not only involves the survival of the species, but also the individual well-being and integrity of each captive animal.

Research plays a key role in the ethical debate over captivity. Elephants in captivity provide unique opportunities to study their behavior, physiology and health, contributing to the understanding and therefore conservation of the species in the wild.

Sin embargo, el desafío ético radica en garantizar que la investigación se realice de manera ética y que los elefantes involucrados se beneficien de estas contribuciones a la ciencia.

La reproducción en cautiverio es otro aspecto que requiere un examen ético detenido. Si bien puede contribuir a la preservación de la especie, debe realizarse con un enfoque centrado en el bienestar de los animales involucrados. Las prácticas éticas en la reproducción en cautiverio incluyen la consideración del espacio disponible, la salud reproductiva y el cuidado adecuado de las crías.

Los programas de liberación son una estrategia que busca reintroducir elefantes criados en cautiverio en entornos naturales. Si bien esta iniciativa tiene el objetivo loable de aumentar las poblaciones salvajes, también plantea interrogantes éticas sobre la preparación de los elefantes para la vida silvestre y la probabilidad de una reintegración exitosa.

Con el crecimiento de la conciencia sobre las consideraciones éticas en el cautiverio de elefantes, se ha generado un impulso significativo hacia innovaciones y mejoras continuas en la gestión de estas poblaciones cautivas.

This paradigm shift not only reflects a deeper understanding of the importance of captive elephant welfare, but also highlights the constant need for evolution in this area to ensure an ethical and sustainable balance.

Firstly, there is a shift towards more ethical approaches in the management of captive populations. Keepers and institutions are adopting practices that prioritize the physical and mental well-being of elephants, recognizing the importance of providing environments that encourage natural behaviors and allow autonomous choices.

These ethical approaches translate into the implementation of measures that reduce stress, promote cognitive and social stimulation, and offer conditions that more closely resemble natural environments.

Furthermore, the development of innovative technologies is playing a crucial role in improving the quality of life of captive elephants. Advances in monitoring technology, for example, allow for more accurate tracking of elephant health and behavior, facilitating more personalized and timely veterinary care.

The use of environmental enrichment technologies is also on the rise, providing elephants with additional opportunities for mental and physical stimulation.

The introduction of enriched habitats, which closely mimic natural conditions, is another area where significant evolution has occurred. Creating environments that allow elephants to express natural behaviors, such as climbing and exploring, contributes to the overall well-being and sense of autonomy of these captive animals.

In this chapter, we have undertaken a comprehensive journey to explore elephant captivity from various ethical perspectives. We have unraveled the complexity of decisions related to welfare and conservation, considering innovations in the management of captive populations and critically examining the ethical implications in elephant captivity.

As we reflect on previous chapters, we have shed light on the delicate balance between preserving the species and respecting the individuality of each captive elephant.

Chapter 10
Hope for the Future

Over time, elephant conservation has undergone significant evolution, adopting more holistic and science-based approaches. Diversified initiatives, ranging from protecting key habitats to combating poaching and promoting human-elephant coexistence, have emerged as critical elements in safeguarding these majestic creatures.

This change in perspective not only reflects a greater understanding of the complexities of conservation, but also highlights the urgent need to address challenges from multiple fronts.

Protecting key habitats has become a cornerstone of conservation efforts. Understanding the importance of maintaining intact natural environments is essential to ensure the survival of elephants and biodiversity in general. 104

Effective conservation goes beyond the mere preservation of a species; it's about maintaining healthy ecosystems in which elephants play essential roles.

The fight against poaching has reached an unprecedented level in terms of sophistication and coordination. Efforts to stop the killing of elephants for their ivory tusks have involved the deployment of specialized patrols, the use of advanced monitoring technologies and international collaboration.

These comprehensive approaches seek not only to protect individual elephants but also to dismantle the criminal networks that drive the illegal ivory trade.

Promoting human-elephant coexistence is another essential dimension of modern conservation. As the boundaries between natural habitats and human communities become intertwined, challenges of conflict arise.

Strategies that seek a balance between the needs of elephants and local communities are essential to ensure harmonious and sustainable coexistence.

These efforts not only focus on preserving specific species, but also maintaining the health of ecosystems as a whole. The understanding that elephants play a crucial role in regulating ecosystems, from seed dispersal to landscape modification, highlights the importance of protecting them as guardians of biodiversity.

Growing global awareness of the vital importance of elephants in the planet's ecology has triggered a notable increase in public participation.

In today's era, information flows rapidly through various platforms, and the instant connection between people around the world has allowed concerns about elephant conservation to be spread effectively.

This phenomenon has given rise to a number of positive developments, with awareness campaigns, conservation movements and citizen pressure emerging as driving forces for significant change.

Awareness campaigns have played a crucial role in informing the public about the challenges facing elephants and highlighting the urgent need for conservation measures.

Through various media, from social networks to advertising campaigns, information has been disseminated about poaching, habitat loss and other problems that affect these majestic animals. This awareness has generated empathy and a deeper understanding of the importance of protecting elephants in the minds of society.

Conservation movements have flourished as organized responses to the threats facing elephants.

Non-governmental organizations, advocacy groups and activists have worked tirelessly to advocate for more robust conservation policies and to generate financial support for the protection of key habitats and the implementation of anti-poaching measures.

These efforts have contributed to significant changes in public and government perception about the importance of preserving elephants.

Citizen pressure has been an essential catalyst to drive changes in government policies. As more people come together to express concern for the survival of elephants, governments have responded by implementing stricter regulations, strengthening enforcement of anti-poaching laws, and committing to more sustainable practices in terms of habitat management and conservation.

Advances in scientific and technological research are playing a crucial and revolutionary role in the understanding and conservation of elephants. Modern science has provided a diverse set of tools that allow scientists to delve into the lives of these majestic animals in ways previously unimaginable.

From satellite monitoring to genetic studies, these technological innovations have opened new frontiers in the study of elephants, providing deeper insight into their ecology, behavior and conservation challenges.

Satellite monitoring has emerged as a powerful tool to track the movements and migrations of elephant herds in real time. This advanced technology allows researchers to follow migratory routes, identify key feeding areas and map critical habitats.

Access to this information in real time not only helps in understanding the ecology of elephants, but also facilitates informed decision making in terms of conservation.

Genetic studies have revealed invaluable information about the genetic diversity and structure of elephant populations.

By analyzing DNA, scientists can identify family relationships, assess the health of populations, and better understand reproductive dynamics. These genetic data are essential for developing conservation strategies that preserve genetic diversity and avoid inbreeding, crucial for the long-term survival of elephant populations.

Imaging techniques, such as trapping photography and video cameras, offer a unique window to observe natural elephant behavior without human interference.

These images capture intimate moments of pack life, providing a deeper understanding of social interactions, movement patterns and emotional expressions. This unique perspective is essential for designing conservation strategies that respect and preserve the complexities of elephant life.

Artificial intelligence and machine learning are also being applied to analyze large data sets collected over time. These advanced technologies allow the identification of complex patterns in elephant behavior and facilitate the prediction of possible threats or changes in the environment.

Integrating these technological tools into elephant research and conservation represents a significant step towards more proactive and adaptive approaches.

Ethical elephant captivity is in a process of positive transformation and constant evolution. Ethical sanctuaries and zoos are leading this change by adopting practices that put the well-being and integrity of captive elephants at the center.

In this emerging paradigm, various strategies are being implemented with the goal of providing healthier and more enriching environments for these majestic beings, while simultaneously advocating for public awareness and education.

First, ethical sanctuaries are redefining the norms of captivity by seeking environments that more closely resemble elephants' natural habitat. These refuges seek to provide expansive areas, allowing elephants to express natural behaviors, such as grazing, playing and socializing.

In addition, innovative environmental enrichment approaches are being implemented, such as the introduction of natural elements and structures that stimulate the elephants' minds, contributing to their physical and emotional well-being.

The promotion of ethics education is another fundamental aspect of this change. Ethical zoos and sanctuaries are committed to providing accurate and understandable information about elephants, their habitats, and the importance of conservation.

Educational programs without compromising animal welfare seek to raise visitors' awareness of the challenges elephants face in the wild and foster greater connection and empathy towards these impressive beings.

Additionally, the implementation of ethical management practices is essential in these locations. Methods based on reward and positive reinforcement are being preferred over outdated and coercive techniques. These respectful approaches allow elephants to voluntarily participate in medical care and daily activities, strengthening the relationship between caregivers and animals.

Continued research in the field of animal welfare also contributes to transformations in ethical captivity. Welfare assessment protocols are being developed that allow for a deeper understanding of the individual needs of elephants, facilitating the adaptation of environments and practices to optimize their quality of life.

Education, without a doubt, remains an essential and powerful tool in forging a sustainable future for elephants. Beyond passing on information about these majestic animals, education plays a critical role in cultivating understanding, respect, and empathy for them from an early age. This approach not only nurtures the relationship between humans and elephants, but also lays the foundation for long-term conservation and harmonious coexistence.

Starting education about the importance of elephants in childhood has a lasting impact. Educational programs designed specifically for children not only convey scientific data and interesting facts about these animals, but also seek to foster an emotional connection and deep appreciation for wildlife.

Early exposure to the wonder and complexity of elephants can sow seeds of interest and curiosity that last throughout life.

Education also plays a vital role in promoting responsible behaviors and decisions in local communities that share habitats with elephants. By understanding the challenges these animals face, people can take more informed steps to mitigate conflicts, engage in sustainable agricultural practices, and contribute to the protection of crucial habitats. This local awareness is essential to ensure peaceful and sustainable coexistence.

Additionally, education provides effective tools to combat poaching and the illegal ivory trade. By informing communities about the devastating consequences of these practices, public support can be mobilized against elephant exploitation and encourage a change in attitudes towards conservation.

Technology and media play a key role in spreading elephant education globally. Documentaries, educational applications, online platforms and social networks allow the sharing of impactful stories, scientific research and educational messages to a global audience.

Although we see a hopeful future for elephant conservation, we cannot ignore that significant challenges remain that require immediate attention and continued commitment.

Among these challenges, habitat loss stands out as an ongoing threat to elephant populations. The expansion of urban areas and the conversion of land for agriculture has drastically reduced elephants' natural habitats, creating conflicts with local communities and limiting their migration routes.

Climate change also represents an increasingly pressing threat. Elephants depend on predictable weather patterns and the availability of natural resources, such as water and food. Disturbances in these patterns can have devastating effects on the distribution and availability of resources, increasing pressure on elephant populations and exacerbating the challenges they face to survive.

Human-elephant interaction remains a critical concern. In regions where elephants and communities share spaces, competition for resources, especially in areas with limited living space, can generate conflicts.

It is clear that addressing these challenges requires collective commitment at a global level. Individuals, communities, governments and organizations must join together in concerted efforts to conserve remaining elephant habitats, implement climate change adaptation measures, and develop effective strategies for harmonious coexistence between humans and elephants.

The role of research and innovation is also fundamental in this process. Better understanding elephants' behavioral patterns, their ecology, and the specific threats they face allows for the development of more effective and adaptive conservation strategies. The application of advanced technologies, such as satellite monitoring and evidence-based conflict mitigation methods, can make a difference in the long-term protection of these majestic creatures.

In this epic journey through the vast plains of the life, history and future of elephants, we have immersed ourselves in a story full of wonders and challenges that have shaped their existence. However, the destiny of these majestic beings is not a simple concluded chapter, but a call to action that resonates at the heart of each page.

The glow of hope for the future lights in our collective hands, lies in the decisions we make today, and reverberates in the unwavering commitment to safeguarding the rich diversity of life on Earth. By advocating for sustainable practices, raising our voices for conservation, and preserving the fragile balance that sustains this fascinating world, we can ensure that elephants, with their unmatched majesty, continue to be the custodians of nature for generations yet to come.

This is not simply the closing of a book, but the prelude to a lasting commitment. The responsibility lies in our hands to write the next chapter, one where the beauty of elephants is intertwined with the preservation of their habitat.

Prepare to forge a future where elephants reign in the fullness of their splendor and where their grandeur is a living tribute to the magnificence of life on Earth!

Dear readers,

As I come to the end of this exciting journey through the pages that chronicle the life and greatness of elephants, I feel deeply grateful for their company on this journey. In each line, we have explored the wonders of these majestic beings, facing the challenges that threaten their existence and celebrating the hope that lies in our hands.

The glow of hope for the future shines before us, a flame that burns in our collective hands. Every word written, every reflection shared, is a reminder of the responsibility we share as guardians of the rich diversity of life on Earth.

In every decision we make today, in every act of advocacy for sustainable practices, we raise our voices in defense of conservation and preserve the delicate balance that sustains this fascinating world.

This is not simply the closing of a book, but the prelude to a lasting commitment. In our hands lies the pen that will write the next chapter, one where the beauty of elephants is intertwined with the preservation of their habitat.

May this legacy, woven from the fibers of ancient wisdom and natural magnificence, inspire meaningful action and awaken a future where elephants walk free and in peace.

Prepare to forge a tomorrow where elephants reign in the fullness of their splendor, where their greatness is a living tribute to the magnificence of life on Earth. May every step we take on this path be guided by the responsibility of being custodians of nature, ensuring that the footprint of the elephants resonates as an eternal echo in the vast landscapes of existence.

With gratitude and hope,

Juan Pimentel

DISCOVER THE LIBRARY
Juan Pimentel

9 798323 927999